Unleashing Your Visual Identity: Harnessing the Power of a Recognizable Image

Fletcher Kyree

Copyright © [2023]

Title: Unleashing Your Visual Identity: Harnessing the Power of a Recognizable Image
Author's: Fletcher Kyree

This book was printed and published by [Publisher's: **Fletcher Kyree**] in [2023]

ISBN:

TABLE OF CONTENT

Chapter 4: Implementing Your Visual Identity Across Various Platforms

Chapter 5: Maintaining and Evolving Your Visual Identity

Chapter 6: Leveraging the Power of Your Visual Identity

Chapter 7: Case Studies: Successful Visual Identity Examples

Examining Iconic Personal Visual Identities

Analyzing Successful Corporate Visual Identities

Drawing Inspiration from Various Industries

Chapter 8: Overcoming Challenges and Pitfalls in Visual Identity Creation

Common Mistakes to Avoid

Addressing Budget Constraints

Navigating Design Trends and Timelessness

Chapter 9: Future Trends in Visual Identity

Emerging Technologies and Their Impact on Visual Identity

The Influence of Social Media on Visual Identity

Predictions and Forecasts for Visual Identity in the Digital Age

Chapter 10: Conclusion: Embracing Your Unique Visual Identity 65

Chapter 1: Understanding the Importance of Visual Identity

The Role of Visual Identity in Personal and Professional Success

Visual identity plays a significant role in both personal and professional success. In a world filled with constant stimuli and information overload, it has become crucial to establish a recognizable image that sets you apart from the crowd. Whether you are an individual looking to make a lasting impression or a professional aiming to enhance your career prospects, harnessing the power of visual identity can make all the difference.

Creating a recognizable image holds immense power. It allows you to showcase your unique personality, values, and strengths, making it easier for others to remember and identify you. Think about some of the most successful individuals or brands you admire – they all have a distinct visual identity that sets them apart. By developing your own visual identity, you can leave a lasting impression on people's minds, which can open doors to new opportunities and forge meaningful connections.

In the professional realm, a strong visual identity can significantly boost your career prospects. It helps you stand out in a competitive job market, making it easier for potential employers to remember and consider you for opportunities. A carefully crafted visual identity can communicate professionalism, creativity, and attention to detail, all of which are highly valued in the workplace. Additionally, a recognizable image can also improve your personal brand, positioning you as an expert in your field and attracting clients or collaborators who resonate with your visual identity.

On a personal level, visual identity can enhance self-confidence, allowing you to express your true self and project an image that aligns with your values and aspirations. It enables you to establish a strong personal brand that reflects who you are and what you stand for. Moreover, a well-defined visual identity can help you navigate social situations with ease, as it gives others an immediate sense of your personality and interests.

In conclusion, the power of creating a recognizable image should not be underestimated. Whether you are looking to achieve personal or professional success, developing a visual identity that represents your unique qualities is key. By harnessing the power of visual identity, you can leave a lasting impression, open doors to new opportunities, and project an image that aligns with your goals and aspirations. So, take the time to explore and unleash your visual identity – it may be the key to unlocking your true potential.

The Psychological Impact of Visual Identity

In today's fast-paced world, where attention spans are decreasing and competition is ever-increasing, it has become crucial for individuals and businesses alike to harness the power of a recognizable image. Visual identity plays a significant role in shaping our perceptions and influencing our behavior. This subchapter delves into the psychological impact of visual identity, exploring the ways in which it can shape our thoughts, emotions, and actions.

At its core, visual identity is about creating a distinct and memorable image that captures the essence of who we are or what our brand represents. It is a powerful tool that allows us to communicate our values, personality, and unique selling proposition in a single glance. But why does visual identity hold such sway over our minds?

One key reason lies in the way our brains process information. Studies have shown that the human brain processes visual information much faster than text or auditory stimuli. When we encounter a visual identity that resonates with us, our brains create an instant connection. This connection triggers an emotional response, which can range from excitement and curiosity to trust and loyalty. By leveraging the power of visual identity, we can tap into these emotional responses and create a lasting impact on our audience.

Furthermore, visual identity plays a crucial role in shaping our perceptions and judgments. Research has shown that people tend to form opinions and make judgments within seconds of encountering a visual stimulus. This phenomenon, known as the "halo effect," suggests that a visually appealing identity can positively influence how others perceive us or our brand. A well-crafted visual identity can create an aura of professionalism, credibility, and trustworthiness, ultimately leading to increased engagement, customer loyalty, and business success.

Moreover, visual identity has the power to evoke specific emotions and associations. Colors, fonts, shapes, and images can all evoke different emotional responses and convey particular messages. For instance, red can evoke a sense of urgency or excitement, while blue may convey trust and calmness. By understanding the psychology behind these visual elements, we can strategically design our visual identity to elicit the desired emotional response from our audience.

In conclusion, the psychological impact of visual identity cannot be underestimated. It has the power to shape our thoughts, emotions, and actions, as well as influence how others perceive us or our brand. By harnessing the power of a recognizable image, we can create a lasting impact, establish a strong brand presence, and ultimately achieve our goals in a visually saturated world. Whether you are an individual looking to make a memorable impression or a business aiming to stand out in a competitive market, understanding the psychological impact of visual identity is essential for success.

Exploring the Elements of Visual Identity

In today's fast-paced world, where information is constantly being thrown at us from every direction, creating a recognizable image has become more important than ever. Whether you are an individual, a small business owner, or a multinational corporation, harnessing the power of visual identity can have a profound impact on your success. This subchapter, titled "Exploring the Elements of Visual Identity," delves into the essential components that make up a strong and memorable visual identity.

First and foremost, a visual identity starts with a logo. Your logo serves as the face of your brand, and it should be distinctive, memorable, and reflective of your values and offerings. Think of successful brands like Apple or Nike – their logos are instantly recognizable and evoke a strong emotional response. It is crucial to invest time and effort in designing a logo that embodies your brand's essence.

Beyond the logo, your chosen color palette plays a significant role in visual identity. Colors have the power to evoke emotions and convey messages without words. Different colors have different meanings and associations, and selecting a palette that aligns with your brand's values and personality can help you establish a strong visual identity. For example, warm tones like red and orange can convey energy and passion, while cool tones like blue and green can evoke feelings of trust and calmness.

Typography is another essential element of visual identity. The fonts you choose for your brand's communication materials – be it your website, marketing materials, or packaging – should be consistent and aligned with your brand's personality. Typography can convey a sense of professionalism, playfulness, or elegance, depending on the chosen font style.

Consistency is the key to a successful visual identity. All elements – from the logo to color palette, typography, and even imagery – should be used consistently across all platforms and channels. This consistency ensures that your brand is instantly recognizable, even at a glance.

In conclusion, exploring the elements of visual identity is crucial for anyone looking to harness the power of a recognizable image. By carefully considering and implementing components such as a distinctive logo, a well-chosen color palette, appropriate typography, and consistent usage, you can create a visual identity that not only captures attention but also leaves a lasting impression. Whether you are an individual or a business, embracing these elements will help you stand out in a crowded marketplace and establish a strong and memorable brand presence.

Chapter 2: Establishing a Strong Foundation for Your Visual Identity

Identifying Your Personal or Brand Values

In today's fast-paced and highly competitive world, it has become more important than ever to create a recognizable image for yourself or your brand. Whether you are an individual looking to establish a strong personal brand or a business aiming to stand out from the crowd, understanding and identifying your personal or brand values is a crucial step in unleashing your visual identity.

Your values serve as the foundation of your identity and what you stand for. They represent your core beliefs, principles, and ethics. By aligning your visual identity with your values, you can create a powerful and authentic image that resonates with your target audience.

Identifying your personal or brand values is a process that requires introspection and self-reflection. Start by asking yourself what matters most to you or your brand. Is it integrity, innovation, sustainability, or community? Consider the qualities that define you or your brand and write them down.

While identifying your values, it is important to be honest and true to yourself. Don't try to emulate someone else's values or follow trends blindly. Your authenticity is what will set you apart and attract like-minded individuals or customers who share your values.

Once you have identified your values, it is essential to communicate them effectively through your visual identity. Your logo, color palette, typography, and overall design should reflect your values and evoke the desired emotions in your audience. For example, if sustainability is one of your core values, incorporating eco-friendly elements into your visual identity can portray your commitment to the environment.

Additionally, consistency is key when it comes to building a recognizable image. Ensure that your values are consistently communicated across all touchpoints, including your website, social media profiles, packaging, and marketing materials. Consistency not only reinforces your values but also helps create a strong and memorable visual identity that people can easily recognize and associate with your brand.

In conclusion, identifying your personal or brand values is a crucial step in unleashing your visual identity. By understanding what you stand for and aligning your visual identity with your values, you can create a powerful and authentic image that resonates with your target audience. Remember to be true to yourself or your brand, communicate your values effectively, and maintain consistency in order to establish a recognizable image that sets you apart in the competitive marketplace.

Defining Your Target Audience

Understanding the importance of defining your target audience is crucial in harnessing the power of a recognizable image. In today's saturated market, it is essential to have a clear understanding of who your audience is, their needs, and how your visual identity can resonate with them. This subchapter will delve into the process of defining your target audience and why it is a vital step in unleashing your visual identity.

One of the key reasons for defining your target audience is to ensure that your visual identity connects with the right people. By understanding who your audience is, you can tailor your image to appeal directly to them, creating a stronger and more meaningful connection. Whether you are a business, artist, or influencer, identifying your target audience will help you attract the right kind of attention and build a loyal following.

To define your target audience, start by conducting thorough market research. This involves analyzing demographics, psychographics, and understanding the unique characteristics of your potential customers. By gathering data on age, gender, location, interests, and values, you can create a detailed profile of your ideal audience. This profile will serve as a foundation for developing your visual identity.

Once you have defined your target audience, it is important to tailor your visual identity to align with their preferences and needs. This includes selecting colors, fonts, and imagery that resonate with your audience and evoke the desired emotions. For example, if your target audience is young and vibrant, you may choose bold and energetic colors, while a more sophisticated audience may respond better to a sleek and minimalist visual style.

Furthermore, understanding your target audience allows you to craft a message that speaks directly to their desires and pain points. By addressing their specific needs, you can establish a strong connection and position yourself as an authority in your niche. Your visual identity should reflect this message, conveying a clear and compelling story that resonates with your audience.

In conclusion, defining your target audience is a crucial step in unleashing the power of a recognizable image. By understanding who your audience is and tailoring your visual identity to their preferences and needs, you can create a strong and meaningful connection. Through market research and a detailed audience profile, you can develop a visual identity that attracts the right kind of attention and builds a loyal following. So, take the time to define your target audience and watch as your visual identity becomes a powerful tool in capturing the hearts and minds of your desired audience.

Conducting Market Research and Competitor Analysis

In today's fast-paced and highly competitive business landscape, establishing a recognizable image is crucial for success. Whether you are an entrepreneur, a small business owner, or a marketing professional, understanding the power of creating a recognizable image can give you a significant edge in the market. To achieve this, conducting thorough market research and competitor analysis is an essential first step.

Market research involves gathering and analyzing data about your target audience, their preferences, and their buying behavior. By understanding your customers' needs and desires, you can tailor your visual identity to resonate with them effectively. This research can be done through surveys, interviews, focus groups, or by analyzing existing data from various sources like social media, industry reports, and market trends.

Competitor analysis, on the other hand, involves studying your competitors' visual identities, marketing strategies, and positioning in the market. This analysis allows you to identify gaps in the market and differentiate yourself from the competition. By examining what works and what doesn't for your competitors, you can develop a unique visual identity that stands out and appeals to your target audience.

To conduct effective market research and competitor analysis, it is crucial to establish clear objectives and a research plan. Define the specific information you need to gather and set realistic timelines for data collection and analysis. When analyzing competitors, focus not only on direct competitors but also on businesses that target similar audiences or offer similar products or services.

Once you have gathered the necessary data, it's time to interpret and apply it to your visual identity. This involves identifying key themes, colors, symbols, and design elements that align with your target audience's preferences and differentiate you from your competitors. This process may require collaboration with graphic designers, marketing professionals, or branding experts to ensure your visual identity effectively communicates your brand values and resonates with your audience.

Remember, creating a recognizable image is not a one-time effort; it requires continuous monitoring and adaptation. Stay updated on market trends, customer feedback, and changes in your competitive landscape. Regularly evaluate and refine your visual identity to stay relevant and maintain a competitive edge in your industry.

By conducting thorough market research and competitor analysis, you can unleash the power of a recognizable image for your business. Understanding your target audience and competition allows you to develop a visual identity that effectively communicates your brand values and differentiates you in the market. Invest time and resources in this crucial step, and you will reap the rewards of a strong and recognizable visual identity.

Chapter 3: Crafting Your Visual Identity

Choosing the Right Color Palette

In the world of visual identity, one of the most important aspects is choosing the right color palette. Colors have a profound impact on our emotions, thoughts, and overall perception. They can convey a wide range of messages and evoke specific feelings in the minds of your audience. Understanding the power of color is crucial for creating a recognizable image that resonates with your target audience.

When it comes to selecting a color palette, there are a few key considerations to keep in mind. Firstly, it's important to understand the psychology behind different colors. Each color has its own unique associations and can evoke specific emotions. For example, warm colors like red and orange are often associated with energy, passion, and excitement, while cool colors like blue and green are associated with calmness, trust, and harmony. By understanding these associations, you can choose colors that align with the message you want to convey.

Another important factor to consider is the industry or niche you belong to. Different industries have their own color conventions and associations. For example, the healthcare industry often uses soothing colors like blue and green to convey a sense of trust and reliability, while the food industry often uses warm, appetizing colors like red and yellow to stimulate appetite. By understanding the color preferences of your niche, you can create a visual identity that resonates with your target audience and sets you apart from your competitors.

It's also crucial to consider the versatility and compatibility of your color palette. Your chosen colors should be able to work across various mediums, such as print, digital, and merchandise. They should also be compatible with other elements of your visual identity, such as your logo, typography, and imagery. A cohesive and harmonious color palette will help create a strong and unified brand image.

Lastly, it's important to test your color palette with your target audience. Conducting surveys or focus groups can provide valuable insights into how your chosen colors are perceived and whether they align with your intended message. By involving your audience in the decision-making process, you can ensure that your color palette resonates with them and creates a memorable and recognizable image.

In conclusion, choosing the right color palette is a crucial step in creating a recognizable image. By understanding the psychology of color, considering industry conventions, ensuring versatility and compatibility, and testing with your target audience, you can create a visually appealing and impactful visual identity that resonates with your audience and sets you apart from the competition.

Selecting Fonts and Typography

In the fast-paced digital world we live in, creating a recognizable image for your brand has never been more important. It's not just about having a great logo or a catchy tagline; every aspect of your visual identity, including the fonts and typography you choose, plays a crucial role in shaping the perception of your brand.

Fonts and typography have the power to evoke emotions, convey messages, and establish a distinct identity for your brand. They can make your content visually appealing and easy to read, or they can create confusion and disinterest. Therefore, it is essential to carefully select the right fonts and typography that align with your brand's personality and values.

When choosing fonts, consider the overall tone and message you want to communicate. Are you aiming for a modern and minimalistic look or a more traditional and sophisticated feel? Each font has its unique personality and can either enhance or detract from your brand's image. Experiment with different font styles, such as serif, sans-serif, script, and display, to find the one that best represents your brand.

Typography, on the other hand, refers to the arrangement and styling of text. It includes factors like font size, spacing, alignment, and hierarchy. Consistency is key when it comes to typography. Establishing a set of guidelines for font sizes, line spacing, and heading styles ensures a cohesive visual identity across all your brand materials.

Remember that readability should always be a top priority. While it may be tempting to choose fancy or decorative fonts, make sure they are still legible, especially in smaller sizes or on different devices.

Consider the context in which your typography will be used, whether it's on a website, in printed materials, or on social media platforms, and adapt accordingly.

Additionally, accessibility is crucial in today's inclusive society. Ensure that your chosen fonts and typography are accessible to people with visual impairments, such as using alt text for images and providing high contrast options.

In conclusion, selecting the right fonts and typography is a vital step in creating a recognizable image for your brand. By considering the tone, message, and overall readability, you can effectively communicate your brand's personality and values to your target audience.

Creating a Memorable Logo or Symbol

In today's fast-paced world, where attention spans are shorter than ever, creating a memorable logo or symbol is crucial for any individual or organization. A logo is more than just a visual representation; it is the face of your brand, instantly recognizable and communicating your values and identity. In this subchapter, we will explore the power of creating a recognizable image and provide you with practical tips on how to design a logo or symbol that leaves a lasting impression.

The power of creating a recognizable image cannot be understated. A well-designed logo or symbol becomes the visual shorthand for your brand, evoking emotions and memories associated with your products or services. Think about iconic logos like Nike's swoosh or Apple's bitten apple; they have become ingrained in our culture, instantly conveying the values and qualities that these brands represent. A memorable logo or symbol helps you stand out in a crowded market, making it easier for people to remember and choose your brand over others.

So, how do you go about creating a memorable logo or symbol? The first step is to know your brand inside out. Understand your values, mission, and target audience. Your logo should reflect these aspects and resonate with your target audience. Research your competitors and the industry you operate in, ensuring that your logo stands out from the crowd while staying relevant.

Simplicity is key when it comes to logo design. A cluttered or complex logo can confuse and fail to leave a lasting impression. Keep your design clean, uncluttered, and easily recognizable even at small sizes.

Choose colors and fonts that reflect your brand personality and evoke the desired emotions. Experiment with different shapes and symbols that align with your brand's identity and values.

A well-designed logo or symbol should be versatile and scalable. It should look equally good on a website, social media profile, or printed materials. Test your logo across different platforms and sizes to ensure its visual impact remains intact.

Lastly, seek feedback from others. Show your logo to friends, colleagues, and potential customers to gather their opinions and make necessary adjustments. Remember, a logo is not set in stone; it can evolve and adapt over time as your brand grows and changes.

In conclusion, creating a memorable logo or symbol is essential in today's competitive landscape. It is the visual representation of your brand, instantly communicating your values and identity. By following the tips provided in this subchapter, you can unleash the power of a recognizable image, making your brand stand out and leave a lasting impression on your target audience.

Designing a Consistent Visual Style

In today's fast-paced and visually driven world, the power of creating a recognizable image cannot be overstated. Whether you are an individual, a small business owner, or a large corporation, having a consistent visual style is key to establishing a strong brand identity and standing out from the competition. This subchapter will delve into the importance of designing a consistent visual style and provide guidance on how to achieve it.

At its core, a consistent visual style is about creating a cohesive and harmonious look and feel across all your visual elements, including your logo, website, marketing materials, and social media presence. It is the visual language that communicates your brand's personality, values, and unique selling proposition. By designing a consistent visual style, you can ensure that your audience recognizes and connects with your brand instantly.

One of the primary benefits of a consistent visual style is increased brand recognition. When your audience sees your logo or any visual element associated with your brand, they should immediately associate it with your business. This recognition creates trust, loyalty, and familiarity, which are crucial for attracting and retaining customers.

Another advantage of a consistent visual style is professionalism. By presenting a cohesive and polished visual identity, you convey a sense of professionalism and attention to detail. This can be particularly beneficial for small businesses or individuals who want to compete with larger, more established brands.

So, how can you go about designing a consistent visual style? Start by defining your brand's personality and values. What do you want to convey to your audience? Is your brand playful, sophisticated, or trustworthy? Once you have identified these key attributes, you can begin to develop a visual language that aligns with your brand's personality.

Next, create a style guide that outlines the specific colors, fonts, and imagery that will be used consistently across all your visual elements. This guide will act as a reference for anyone involved in creating or using your brand's visuals, ensuring that there is a unified and cohesive look and feel.

Finally, regularly review and update your visual style to ensure it remains relevant and resonates with your target audience. Design trends and consumer preferences evolve over time, so it's important to stay up to date and adapt accordingly.

In conclusion, designing a consistent visual style is a powerful tool for establishing a recognizable image and attracting your target audience. By creating a cohesive and harmonious visual language, you can increase brand recognition, convey professionalism, and ultimately drive business success. So, take the time to invest in your visual identity and unleash the power of a recognizable image.

Chapter 4: Implementing Your Visual Identity Across Various Platforms

Creating a Cohesive Website Design

In today's digital age, having a strong online presence is essential for businesses and individuals alike. One of the key elements in building an effective online brand is creating a cohesive website design. A well-designed website not only attracts visitors but also leaves a lasting impression and helps in building a recognizable image.

The power of creating a recognizable image cannot be overstated. It distinguishes your brand from the competition and helps to establish trust and credibility with potential customers. When it comes to your website design, consistency is key. A cohesive design ensures that all aspects of your website, from the color scheme to the typography and layout, work together harmoniously to create a memorable and visually appealing experience for your visitors.

To begin creating a cohesive website design, start by defining your brand identity. Consider your target audience, values, and unique selling proposition. This will provide a foundation for the visual elements of your website design. Choose colors, fonts, and imagery that reflect your brand persona and resonate with your target audience.

Consistency in design elements is crucial for creating a recognizable image. Use the same color palette throughout your website to build brand recognition. Select fonts that are easy to read and align with your brand personality. Ensure that your logo is prominently displayed and consistent across all pages.

In addition to visual consistency, pay attention to the layout and navigation of your website. A well-organized and intuitive layout makes it easy for visitors to find the information they are looking for and enhances their overall user experience. Use clear and concise headings, and make sure that your navigation menu is easily accessible and user-friendly.

Lastly, incorporate your brand's story and messaging into your website design. Use compelling content and visuals to communicate your brand's values, mission, and unique selling points. This will help to build a connection with your audience and differentiate your brand from others in your niche.

In conclusion, creating a cohesive website design is essential for harnessing the power of a recognizable image. By defining your brand identity, maintaining visual consistency, optimizing your layout and navigation, and incorporating your brand's story, you can create a website that stands out and leaves a lasting impression on your visitors. Remember, a cohesive website design not only enhances your brand's image but also plays a vital role in attracting and retaining customers in today's competitive online landscape.

Designing Eye-Catching Business Cards and Stationery

In today's highly competitive business landscape, creating a recognizable image is essential for success. Your visual identity is a powerful tool that can leave a lasting impression on potential clients and customers. One of the most effective ways to showcase your brand is through eye-catching business cards and stationery. These small but impactful marketing tools can convey your professionalism, creativity, and attention to detail.

When designing business cards and stationery, it is important to consider the following elements:

1. Logo and Branding: Your business cards and stationery should prominently feature your logo and adhere to your brand guidelines. Consistency is key in creating a recognizable image.

2. Typography: Choose fonts that align with your brand's personality and are easy to read. Experiment with different font combinations to create a visually appealing design.

3. Color Scheme: Select colors that reflect your brand's identity and evoke the desired emotions. Use colors strategically to highlight important information and create visual hierarchy.

4. Layout and Composition: A well-designed layout can make your business cards and stationery stand out. Consider the placement of your logo, contact information, and any additional design elements. White space is important for creating a clean and professional look.

5. Paper Quality: Invest in high-quality paper stock that feels substantial and luxurious. The tactile experience of your business cards and stationery can leave a lasting impression on recipients.

6. Unique Design Elements: Consider incorporating die-cutting, embossing, or foil stamping techniques to add visual interest and make your business cards and stationery memorable.

Remember, your business cards and stationery are not just tools for sharing contact information. They are an extension of your brand and an opportunity to showcase your professionalism and creativity. Don't be afraid to think outside the box and create unique designs that align with your brand's personality.

In conclusion, designing eye-catching business cards and stationery is an essential part of creating a recognizable image. By paying attention to details such as logo and branding, typography, color scheme, layout and composition, paper quality, and unique design elements, you can create impactful marketing tools that leave a lasting impression on your target audience. Invest time and effort into crafting visually appealing business cards and stationery, and watch as your brand recognition grows.

Developing Engaging Social Media Profiles

In today's digital age, social media has become an integral part of our lives. It has transformed the way we communicate, connect, and share information. With millions of users across various platforms, it has become essential for individuals and businesses alike to create engaging social media profiles. This subchapter explores the power of developing a recognizable image on social media platforms and provides tips on how to effectively do so.

The power of creating a recognizable image on social media cannot be underestimated. It serves as your digital identity and helps you stand out in the crowded online world. Whether you are an individual looking to build your personal brand or a business aiming to attract customers, a strong visual identity is crucial.

To begin developing an engaging social media profile, start by selecting a consistent color palette and design elements that align with your personal or brand identity. This will help create a cohesive look across all your social media platforms and make it easier for your audience to recognize and remember you.

Next, focus on crafting a compelling bio or about section that clearly communicates who you are or what your brand stands for. Use concise and attention-grabbing language to capture the interest of your audience and entice them to explore further.

Another important aspect of developing an engaging social media profile is posting high-quality and visually appealing content. Use high-resolution images, videos, and graphics that are relevant to your niche. Experiment with different formats and styles to keep your audience engaged and interested.

Consistency is key when it comes to maintaining an engaging social media profile. Establish a posting schedule and stick to it. Regularly interact with your audience by responding to comments and messages promptly. Engage in conversations, share valuable insights, and provide useful information to build trust and credibility.

Lastly, don't forget to analyze and evaluate your social media efforts. Use analytics tools provided by the platforms to measure the performance of your posts and identify what works best for your audience. Adjust your strategies accordingly to optimize engagement and reach.

In conclusion, developing engaging social media profiles is essential in today's digital landscape. By creating a recognizable image, you can effectively communicate your personal or brand identity and stand out from the crowd. By following the tips outlined in this subchapter, you will be well on your way to harnessing the power of a recognizable image on social media platforms.

Incorporating Your Visual Identity into Marketing Materials

In today's fast-paced and highly competitive business landscape, creating a recognizable image for your brand has become more important than ever. Your visual identity is not just a logo or a color scheme; it is the essence of your brand and what sets you apart from the competition. It is what your customers instantly recognize and associate with your products or services. In this subchapter, we will delve into the power of incorporating your visual identity into your marketing materials and how it can significantly impact your business.

One of the key advantages of incorporating your visual identity into marketing materials is consistency. When your customers see your logo, colors, and other visual elements consistently across various platforms, it builds trust and familiarity. Consistency creates a strong impression and makes your brand more memorable. By consistently using your visual identity in your marketing materials, you reinforce your brand's message and values, ultimately increasing brand recognition and loyalty.

Another benefit of incorporating your visual identity into marketing materials is differentiation. In a crowded marketplace, standing out from the competition is crucial. Your visual identity helps you differentiate your brand from others, making it easier for customers to identify and choose your products or services. By consistently using your visual identity, you create a unique and recognizable image that sets you apart from the competition.

Moreover, incorporating your visual identity into marketing materials can enhance the overall aesthetic appeal of your campaigns. A visually appealing marketing material has the power to grab attention, engage the audience, and leave a lasting impression. By using your visual identity consistently, you create a cohesive and visually appealing brand image that resonates with your target audience.

Furthermore, incorporating your visual identity into marketing materials also ensures brand recall. When customers see your visual identity repeatedly, it becomes deeply ingrained in their minds. This makes it easier for them to recall your brand when making purchasing decisions. By incorporating your visual identity into marketing materials, you create a strong brand presence that stays with your customers even after they have interacted with your campaigns.

In conclusion, incorporating your visual identity into marketing materials is crucial for creating a recognizable image for your brand. It enhances consistency, differentiation, aesthetic appeal, and brand recall. By harnessing the power of your visual identity and incorporating it into your marketing materials, you can establish a strong brand presence, build customer trust, and ultimately drive business growth.

Chapter 5: Maintaining and Evolving Your Visual Identity

Consistency is Key: Guidelines for Proper Usage

In today's visually saturated world, creating a recognizable image is vital for individuals and businesses alike. The power of a recognizable image lies in its ability to leave a lasting impression and communicate a message without uttering a single word. However, achieving this level of recognition requires a consistent approach to visual identity. In this subchapter, we will delve into the guidelines for proper usage that will help you unleash the full potential of your visual identity.

First and foremost, it is crucial to understand that consistency is the cornerstone of creating a recognizable image. Consistency builds trust and familiarity, allowing your audience to easily identify and connect with your brand. To achieve this, start by defining your brand's visual elements, such as your logo, color palette, typography, and imagery. These elements should be carefully chosen to align with your brand's personality and values.

Once you have established your visual identity, it is essential to apply it consistently across all touchpoints. Whether it be your website, social media profiles, marketing materials, or physical spaces, maintaining a cohesive visual language will reinforce your brand's recognition. This means using your brand's colors and typography consistently, incorporating your logo in a prominent and appropriate manner, and selecting imagery that aligns with your brand's aesthetics.

Furthermore, it is important to consider the scalability of your visual identity. In a world where digital platforms and screen sizes vary greatly, your visual elements should be adaptable and easily recognizable across different mediums. Test the legibility of your logo and typography in various sizes, ensuring they remain clear and impactful. Similarly, optimize your imagery for different platforms while maintaining a consistent visual style.

Lastly, remember that consistency extends beyond visual elements. It also includes the tone and messaging you use to communicate with your audience. Consistently applying your brand's voice and values in your communication will strengthen the recognition of your visual identity.

In conclusion, creating a recognizable image requires consistency in every aspect of your visual identity. By following the guidelines for proper usage outlined in this subchapter, you can harness the power of a recognizable image to leave a lasting impression on your audience. Remember, consistency is key – it builds trust, reinforces recognition, and sets you apart in today's visually-driven world.

Adapting Your Visual Identity for Different Situations

In today's fast-paced world, establishing a strong visual identity is crucial for individuals and businesses alike. It goes beyond mere aesthetics – a recognizable image has the power to convey your values, establish credibility, and leave a lasting impression. However, it is equally important to adapt your visual identity to different situations and contexts to ensure maximum impact and relevance.

Whether you're an individual building your personal brand or a business crafting your company's image, understanding the importance of adapting your visual identity can make all the difference. This subchapter will delve into the strategies and techniques you can employ to ensure consistency while adjusting to various situations.

First and foremost, it is essential to understand the core elements of your visual identity and how they can be modified without compromising brand recognition. Your logo, color palette, typography, and imagery are the building blocks of your identity. While these elements should remain consistent, their application may need to be adjusted to suit different mediums, platforms, or target audiences.

Consider the power of creating a recognizable image by tailoring it to specific niches. Different niches may require you to adopt a different tone, style, or visual approach. For example, a tech startup targeting a young and tech-savvy audience may opt for vibrant colors and contemporary design elements, while a luxury brand targeting affluent customers might choose a more sophisticated and elegant approach.

Adapting your visual identity also means considering the various touchpoints where your brand interacts with its audience. From websites and social media platforms to print materials and physical spaces, each touchpoint demands a thoughtful adaptation of your visual identity. Consistency across these platforms is vital, yet subtle adjustments can be made to ensure the message resonates with the specific context and audience.

Another crucial aspect of adapting your visual identity is staying relevant in a rapidly changing world. As societal trends, technology, and consumer preferences evolve, your visual identity must evolve alongside them. Regularly conduct market research and analyze your target audience to identify any shifts that may require adjustments to your branding elements.

In conclusion, while establishing a recognizable image is powerful, adapting it to different situations is equally important. By understanding the core elements of your visual identity and making strategic modifications, you can ensure consistency while remaining relevant and impactful. Whether you are an individual or a business, mastering the art of adapting your visual identity will enable you to effectively communicate your values, establish credibility, and leave a lasting impression in any situation.

Rebranding Strategies and Considerations

In today's fast-paced and ever-evolving marketplace, staying relevant and capturing the attention of your target audience is crucial. One powerful tool that can help you achieve this is creating a recognizable image through effective branding. By leveraging the power of branding, you can establish a strong and lasting connection with your audience, differentiate yourself from competitors, and ultimately drive growth and success for your business.

Rebranding is a strategic process that involves refreshing or completely overhauling your brand's visual identity to reflect your evolving values, goals, and target market. It is a powerful tool that can breathe new life into your business and propel it to new heights. However, before embarking on a rebranding journey, there are several key considerations and strategies to keep in mind.

First and foremost, it is essential to conduct thorough research and analysis to understand your target audience, their preferences, and their perception of your current brand. This will help you identify areas for improvement and guide your rebranding efforts effectively. Additionally, understanding your competitors and industry trends will allow you to stand out and position your brand uniquely.

Another crucial aspect of rebranding is establishing a clear and compelling brand story. Your visual identity should align with your brand's narrative, values, and mission, helping to create an emotional connection with your audience. By telling a compelling story through your visual elements, you can evoke positive emotions and build trust, loyalty, and customer engagement.

When considering rebranding, it is important to strike a balance between maintaining consistency and embracing change. While it is essential to retain some elements that your audience associates with your brand, such as colors or logos, it is equally vital to infuse new elements that reflect your brand's evolution. This will signal growth and innovation, capturing the attention of both existing and potential customers.

Lastly, rebranding should not be seen as a one-time task but as an ongoing process. Regularly evaluating and refining your visual identity will ensure that it remains relevant and resonates with your target market. It is essential to stay adaptable and responsive to changes in consumer preferences, technology, and industry trends to maintain a strong and recognizable image.

In conclusion, rebranding is a powerful tool that can help your business thrive in today's competitive landscape. By carefully considering your target audience, establishing a compelling brand story, and embracing both consistency and change, you can create a recognizable image that captivates and resonates with your audience. Remember, successful rebranding is an ongoing process, requiring adaptability and a keen understanding of your market. So, unleash the power of your visual identity and watch your business soar to new heights.

Chapter 6: Leveraging the Power of Your Visual Identity

Building Trust and Recognition with a Strong Visual Identity

In today's fast-paced and highly competitive world, establishing a strong visual identity is crucial for individuals and businesses alike. Your visual identity serves as a representation of your brand, and it has the power to build trust and recognition among your target audience. This subchapter explores the importance of creating a recognizable image and the immense benefits it can bring to everyone, regardless of their industry or profession.

One of the key advantages of having a recognizable image is that it helps in establishing trust with your audience. When people see a consistent visual identity associated with your brand, they begin to develop a sense of familiarity and reliability. This trust is vital for any individual or business, as it lays the foundation for long-term relationships and repeat customers.

Furthermore, a strong visual identity allows you to stand out in a crowded marketplace. In today's digital age, where attention spans are dwindling, having a distinctive and memorable image is essential for capturing the attention of potential customers. It helps you differentiate yourself from competitors and create a lasting impression in the minds of your target audience.

Creating a recognizable image also fosters brand loyalty. When customers are able to easily identify your brand through its visual identity, they are more likely to choose your products or services over others. This loyalty not only generates repeat business but also leads to positive word-of-mouth referrals, further expanding your customer base.

Another benefit of a strong visual identity is its ability to communicate your values and personality. Through the use of colors, fonts, and graphics, you can convey the essence of your brand and connect with your audience on a deeper level. This emotional connection creates a sense of belonging and fosters brand advocacy, as customers feel aligned with your values.

While building a recognizable image may seem like a daunting task, it is well worth the effort. From individuals looking to establish a personal brand to businesses aiming to make a mark in their industry, a strong visual identity has the power to set you apart and drive long-term success.

In conclusion, creating a recognizable image is a powerful tool that can benefit everyone. It builds trust, helps you stand out, fosters brand loyalty, and communicates your values. By harnessing the power of a strong visual identity, you can unleash your full potential and achieve your goals in today's visually-driven world.

Using Visual Identity to Strengthen Your Personal or Brand Story

In today's fast-paced and highly competitive world, it has become increasingly important to stand out and make a lasting impression. Whether you are an individual looking to establish a strong personal brand or a business aiming to create a unique identity, harnessing the power of a recognizable visual identity is crucial. This subchapter will explore the various ways in which visual identity can be used to strengthen your personal or brand story.

A recognizable image has the power to convey a multitude of messages and emotions, often in an instant. It can evoke a sense of trust, professionalism, and reliability, making it easier for people to connect with you or your brand. By carefully crafting your visual identity, you can shape the narrative surrounding your personal or brand story, influencing how others perceive and engage with you.

One of the key benefits of creating a recognizable visual identity is that it helps you establish a sense of consistency and coherence across all touchpoints. From your logo and color scheme to typography and imagery, each element should work together to create a cohesive visual language. This consistency not only enhances your credibility but also helps to build brand recognition, making it easier for people to identify and remember you.

Furthermore, a strong visual identity allows you to differentiate yourself from competitors. By carefully considering your target audience and understanding their preferences, you can design a visual identity that resonates with them and sets you apart. This distinctiveness can be a powerful tool in capturing attention and building a loyal customer base.

In the age of social media and digital marketing, a strong visual identity is even more vital. Eye-catching visuals are more likely to be shared and remembered, increasing your reach and visibility. By incorporating your visual identity into your online presence, such as your website, social media profiles, and digital advertisements, you can ensure a consistent and memorable brand experience for your audience.

In conclusion, harnessing the power of a recognizable visual identity is essential for both individuals and brands. By creating a cohesive and distinctive visual language, you can strengthen your personal or brand story, enhance credibility, differentiate yourself from competitors, and increase visibility. Investing time and effort into developing a strong visual identity is a wise decision that will yield long-term benefits.

Maximizing the Impact of Visual Identity in Marketing and Advertising

In today's fast-paced and highly competitive business world, creating a strong and recognizable visual identity is more important than ever before. A well-crafted visual identity has the power to grab the attention of potential customers, evoke emotions, and leave a lasting impression. It is the key to standing out from the crowd and establishing a unique brand identity.

The power of creating a recognizable image cannot be underestimated. When consumers see a visual identity that they can easily identify and associate with a particular brand, it creates a sense of familiarity and trust. This familiarity builds brand loyalty and increases the chances of repeat purchases. In fact, studies have shown that consumers are more likely to choose a brand they recognize over one they don't, even if the unknown brand offers a superior product or service.

Visual identity goes beyond just a logo. It encompasses the entire visual representation of a brand, including colors, typography, imagery, and even the overall design aesthetic. All these elements work together to create a cohesive and memorable brand image that resonates with the target audience.

To maximize the impact of visual identity in marketing and advertising, it is important to ensure consistency across all channels and touchpoints. Whether it's a website, social media platform, or print advertisement, the visual identity should be instantly recognizable and consistent in its execution. This consistency builds trust and reinforces the brand's message and values.

Another important aspect of maximizing the impact of visual identity is understanding the target audience. Different demographics respond differently to various visual cues. By conducting market research and understanding consumer preferences, businesses can tailor their visual identity to better resonate with their target audience. This includes choosing colors and imagery that evoke the desired emotions and using typography that is legible and appropriate for the brand's personality.

In conclusion, a strong and recognizable visual identity is a powerful tool in marketing and advertising. It helps businesses differentiate themselves from the competition, build brand loyalty, and leave a lasting impression on consumers. By maximizing the impact of visual identity through consistency and understanding the target audience, businesses can harness the power of a recognizable image and take their marketing efforts to new heights.

Chapter 7: Case Studies: Successful Visual Identity Examples

Examining Iconic Personal Visual Identities

In today's fast-paced world, creating a recognizable image has become more important than ever. Whether you are an individual looking to establish a personal brand or a business aiming to stand out from the competition, a visual identity plays a crucial role in capturing attention and leaving a lasting impression. This subchapter will delve into the concept of iconic personal visual identities, exploring the power they hold and the impact they can have on various niches.

The power of creating a recognizable image cannot be underestimated. It enables you to communicate who you are and what you stand for, even before a single word is spoken. Think about some of the most iconic figures in history - from Steve Jobs in his black turtleneck and blue jeans to Coco Chanel with her timeless little black dress. These individuals created a visual identity that became synonymous with their brand and values.

Examining these iconic personal visual identities can provide valuable insights into what makes them successful. It is not just about wearing a specific outfit or using a particular color scheme, but rather about embodying a consistent image that aligns with your core message. By understanding the elements that contribute to their success, you can apply similar principles to your own visual identity.

Furthermore, this subchapter will explore how different niches can benefit from the power of a recognizable image. Whether you are a freelancer, an entrepreneur, or an artist, having a strong visual identity will help you stand out in a crowded market. It can attract clients, build trust, and establish you as an authority in your field.

Additionally, we will discuss the importance of adapting your visual identity to different platforms and mediums. In today's digital age, it is crucial to have a cohesive image across various channels, including websites, social media profiles, and print materials. Consistency reinforces your brand and ensures that your audience can easily recognize and remember you.

By examining iconic personal visual identities and understanding their impact, you will be equipped with the knowledge and tools to unleash your own visual identity. Whether you are an individual or a business, harnessing the power of a recognizable image can elevate your brand and make a lasting impression on your audience. Stay tuned as we dive deeper into the world of visual identities and discover how you can unleash your own unique image.

Analyzing Successful Corporate Visual Identities

In the competitive world of business, it is essential to create a strong and recognizable visual identity for your company. A well-crafted corporate visual identity can make a lasting impression on your target audience and set you apart from your competitors. This subchapter will delve into the secrets behind successful corporate visual identities, exploring the power they hold and the benefits they can bring to any organization.

One of the key aspects of a successful corporate visual identity is consistency. When customers see your logo, colors, and overall visual style consistently across different platforms, they begin to associate them with your brand. This consistency helps build trust and familiarity, making it easier for your audience to recognize your company and remember it in the future.

Another important factor to consider is simplicity. A successful corporate visual identity is often simple yet impactful. It should be easily understood and recognized by anyone, regardless of their background or knowledge about your industry. By keeping your visual elements clean and uncluttered, you ensure that your message is conveyed effectively and efficiently.

Furthermore, a successful corporate visual identity aligns with the values and personality of your brand. It should accurately reflect who you are as a company and what you stand for. For example, if your brand is known for its eco-friendly practices, your visual identity should incorporate elements that convey sustainability and environmental consciousness.

Analyzing successful corporate visual identities also involves studying the strategies and techniques employed by top companies in different industries. By examining case studies and real-life examples, you can gain valuable insights into the thought processes and decisions that led to their success. This knowledge can then be applied to your own corporate visual identity, helping you create a powerful and effective image for your brand.

The benefits of creating a recognizable image for your company are vast. A well-crafted visual identity can help you attract new customers, build brand loyalty, and increase your market share. It can also give you a competitive edge in the industry, as customers are more likely to choose a brand they recognize and trust.

In conclusion, analyzing successful corporate visual identities is a crucial step in creating a strong and recognizable image for your brand. By understanding the power and benefits of a well-crafted visual identity, you can make informed decisions and create a lasting impression on your target audience. So, whether you are a small startup or a multinational corporation, investing in your visual identity is key to unleashing your brand's full potential.

Drawing Inspiration from Various Industries

In today's competitive world, creating a recognizable image is essential for individuals, businesses, and organizations. The power of a visual identity cannot be underestimated, as it serves as a unique representation of who you are and what you stand for. To unleash the potential of your visual identity, it is crucial to draw inspiration from various industries.

Every industry has its own distinct characteristics and visual elements that make it recognizable. By exploring different sectors and studying their visual identities, you can gain valuable insights and ideas to create a unique and memorable image for yourself or your brand.

One industry that excels in visual identity is the fashion industry. Fashion brands are renowned for their ability to create visually stunning and distinct logos, typography, and color schemes. By observing their methods, you can learn how to make your visual identity stand out in a crowded marketplace. Analyze the fashion industry's use of bold and eye-catching designs to capture attention and evoke emotion.

Another industry to draw inspiration from is technology. Tech companies are known for their sleek and modern visual identities. By studying their use of minimalist designs, clean lines, and futuristic color palettes, you can incorporate these elements into your own visual identity to convey a sense of innovation and professionalism.

The entertainment industry is also a great source of inspiration. Movie studios, music labels, and production companies excel in creating visually captivating images that resonate with their target audience. By examining their use of visually appealing graphics, vibrant colors, and dynamic typography, you can learn how to create an image that captivates and engages your audience.

Moreover, it is important to look beyond your immediate industry. Explore other sectors such as food and beverage, automotive, or even architecture. Each industry has its own unique visual language that can provide fresh perspectives and ideas for your visual identity.

Remember, the power of creating a recognizable image lies in the ability to stand out from the crowd. By drawing inspiration from various industries, you can infuse your visual identity with elements that make it distinct, memorable, and impactful. Embrace the creativity and diversity that different industries offer, and let it fuel your journey towards unleashing the power of your visual identity.

Chapter 8: Overcoming Challenges and Pitfalls in Visual Identity Creation

Common Mistakes to Avoid

In the world we live in today, where visual content dominates our everyday lives, it is crucial for individuals and businesses to harness the power of a recognizable image. Your visual identity is not only a reflection of who you are or what your brand represents, but it also serves as a powerful tool to attract and engage your target audience. However, it is important to be aware of the common mistakes that can hinder your efforts in creating a strong visual identity. In this subchapter, we will explore some of these mistakes and provide you with valuable insights on how to avoid them.

One of the most common mistakes people make is trying to imitate others. While it is natural to draw inspiration from successful individuals or brands, it is important to maintain your authenticity and create a unique visual identity that sets you apart from the rest. By imitating others, you risk losing your own voice and diluting your brand's message.

Another mistake to avoid is neglecting consistency. Your visual identity should be consistent across all platforms and mediums. This includes your logo, color palette, typography, and overall design elements. Inconsistency can confuse your audience and make it difficult for them to recognize and remember your brand. Ensure that all your visual elements work harmoniously together to create a cohesive and memorable image.

Furthermore, overlooking the importance of research can be a detrimental mistake. Understanding your target audience is vital in creating a visual identity that resonates with them. Conduct thorough research to gain insights into their preferences, values, and interests. This will enable you to tailor your visual identity to effectively communicate and connect with your audience.

Lastly, many individuals and businesses underestimate the power of professional help. While it may be tempting to design your own logo or create your own visuals, seeking the expertise of a professional designer can make a significant difference. A professional will have the skills and knowledge to create a visually appealing and impactful identity that aligns with your goals and values.

In conclusion, the power of creating a recognizable image cannot be underestimated. However, it is crucial to avoid common mistakes that can hinder your efforts in establishing a strong visual identity. By avoiding imitation, maintaining consistency, conducting thorough research, and seeking professional help when needed, you can unleash the true potential of your visual identity and harness its power to attract and engage your target audience.

Addressing Budget Constraints

In today's competitive business landscape, creating a recognizable image is crucial for success. Your visual identity is your brand's first impression, and it can make or break your business. However, many individuals and companies face the challenge of limited budgets when it comes to developing and implementing a visual identity. In this subchapter, we will explore practical strategies for addressing budget constraints while still harnessing the power of a recognizable image.

1. Define your goals and priorities: Before allocating any budget to your visual identity, it's essential to clearly define your goals and priorities. Are you looking to establish a strong online presence? Do you want to create a consistent brand image across different platforms? By understanding your objectives, you can make informed decisions on where to allocate your limited resources.

2. DIY design tools: Thanks to technological advancements, there are now numerous do-it-yourself (DIY) design tools available at affordable prices or even for free. These tools provide templates, graphics, and customization options, allowing you to create a visually appealing visual identity without the need for professional designers. Platforms like Canva and Adobe Spark are excellent examples of user-friendly tools that can help you unleash your visual identity on a tight budget.

3. Focus on essentials: When working with a limited budget, it's crucial to prioritize the essential elements of your visual identity. Invest in a well-designed logo, color palette, and typography that accurately represent your brand's personality. These elements can be used

consistently across various marketing materials, ensuring a recognizable image even with limited resources.

4. Leverage social media: Social media platforms offer incredible opportunities for brand exposure without breaking the bank. By consistently sharing visually appealing content, engaging with your audience, and utilizing relevant hashtags, you can build a recognizable image and grow your brand organically. Social media platforms also provide cost-effective advertising options, allowing you to reach a wider audience with targeted campaigns.

5. Collaborate with influencers: Influencer marketing has become a powerful tool for establishing brand recognition. Identify influential individuals in your industry who align with your brand values and collaborate with them to promote your visual identity. Influencers often offer flexible pricing options, making it a budget-friendly strategy for boosting brand awareness.

Remember, even with limited resources, it's essential to invest time and effort into developing a recognizable visual identity. By strategically allocating your budget and utilizing cost-effective strategies, you can harness the power of a recognizable image, ultimately driving growth and success for your brand.

In conclusion, addressing budget constraints while creating a recognizable visual identity is possible. By defining your goals, leveraging DIY tools, focusing on essentials, utilizing social media, and collaborating with influencers, you can unleash the power of your brand's visual identity without breaking the bank.

Navigating Design Trends and Timelessness

In the ever-evolving world of design, it can be challenging to strike a balance between following the latest trends and creating a timeless visual identity. In this subchapter, we will explore the importance of navigating design trends while maintaining a recognizable image that stands the test of time. Whether you are an individual seeking to establish a personal brand or a business looking to create a lasting visual identity, understanding the power of design trends and timelessness is essential.

Design trends can be both a blessing and a curse. On one hand, they offer fresh and innovative ideas that can make your visual identity stand out from the crowd. On the other hand, trends can quickly become outdated, leaving your brand looking obsolete. It is crucial to approach design trends with caution and consider how they align with your overall brand message and values.

Creating a recognizable image is the ultimate goal for any individual or business. A recognizable image allows you to establish a strong brand identity and forge a connection with your target audience. It becomes a visual representation of who you are and what you stand for. By harnessing the power of a recognizable image, you can differentiate yourself from competitors and leave a lasting impression on your audience.

Timelessness is the key to longevity in design. While it may be tempting to chase after the latest trends, it is important to remember that what is trendy today may not be relevant tomorrow. By focusing on creating a design that transcends time, you ensure that your visual identity remains relevant and impactful for years to come. This does not mean you should completely ignore trends; instead, use them as inspiration and adapt them to fit your brand's unique style.

To navigate design trends and timelessness successfully, it is crucial to strike a balance between innovation and consistency. Embrace trends that align with your brand's personality and values, but avoid being overly influenced by fleeting fads. Continuously evaluate and refine your visual identity to ensure it remains fresh and relevant, while still maintaining core elements that make it recognizable.

In conclusion, navigating design trends and timelessness is a delicate art. By understanding the power of creating a recognizable image and being mindful of how trends can impact your visual identity, you can create a design that stands the test of time. Remember, trends come and go, but a well-crafted and recognizable image is an investment that will pay off in the long run.

Chapter 9: Future Trends in Visual Identity

Emerging Technologies and Their Impact on Visual Identity

In today's rapidly evolving digital landscape, emerging technologies have revolutionized the way we interact with visual identity. From social media platforms to augmented reality, these technologies have not only transformed the way we communicate, but also the way we perceive and engage with brands. This subchapter explores the profound impact of emerging technologies on visual identity and how businesses can harness their power to create a recognizable image.

One of the most significant advancements in technology is the rise of social media platforms. These platforms have become a breeding ground for visual content, allowing businesses to reach a wider audience and create a strong brand presence. Through compelling visuals, companies can establish a unique and recognizable image that resonates with their target audience. Platforms like Instagram and Pinterest have become essential tools for businesses to showcase their products or services, allowing them to visually communicate their brand's values and personality.

Furthermore, the advent of virtual and augmented reality has opened up exciting possibilities for visual identity. With virtual reality, businesses can create immersive experiences that transport users into a brand's world, enabling them to engage with visuals in a more dynamic and interactive manner. Augmented reality, on the other hand, allows for the seamless integration of digital content into the real world, enabling brands to enhance their visual identity through creative and captivating experiences.

The power of emerging technologies lies in their ability to evoke emotions and create memorable experiences. Whether it's through virtual reality, augmented reality, or even artificial intelligence, businesses can leverage these technologies to leave a lasting impression on their audience. By integrating these technologies into their visual identity, companies can differentiate themselves from competitors and build a strong brand that resonates with their target market.

However, it is crucial for businesses to strike a balance between leveraging emerging technologies and maintaining authenticity. While these technologies can enhance visual identity, they should never overshadow the core values and essence of the brand. The key is to use these technologies as tools to amplify the brand's message and create an emotional connection with the audience.

In conclusion, emerging technologies have revolutionized the way businesses approach visual identity. From the power of social media platforms to the immersive experiences offered by virtual and augmented reality, these technologies have transformed the way brands communicate and engage with their audience. By harnessing the power of emerging technologies, businesses can create a recognizable image that captivates their target market and sets them apart from the competition.

The Influence of Social Media on Visual Identity

In today's digital age, it is undeniable that social media has become an integral part of our lives. It has revolutionized the way we communicate, connect, and share information. But did you know that social media also plays a significant role in shaping and influencing our visual identity?

Visual identity refers to the image, perception, and recognition of a brand or individual. It encompasses elements such as logo, color scheme, typography, and overall design aesthetic. Establishing a strong visual identity is crucial for individuals and brands alike, as it helps differentiate them from their competitors and creates a cohesive and memorable image.

Social media platforms, with their vast reach and ability to disseminate content quickly, have transformed the way visual identity is perceived and consumed. They offer a unique opportunity for individuals and brands to showcase their visual identity and connect with their target audience on a more personal level.

One of the most significant impacts of social media on visual identity is the democratization of design. With the rise of user-friendly design tools and platforms, anyone can now create visually appealing content without the need for professional designers. This has enabled individuals and small businesses to establish a recognizable visual identity, even with limited resources.

Moreover, social media platforms provide a space for individuals and brands to experiment and evolve their visual identity. They serve as a testing ground for different design elements, allowing users to gauge audience response and make necessary adjustments. This dynamic nature of social media has also led to the emergence of trends and aesthetic movements, shaping the overall visual landscape.

Social media's influence on visual identity also extends to the way we perceive authenticity. In an era of curated feeds and carefully crafted images, maintaining an authentic visual identity becomes a challenge. It is imperative for individuals and brands to strike a balance between showcasing their unique personality and meeting audience expectations. Social media users are increasingly craving genuine and relatable content, and visual identity plays a crucial role in delivering this authenticity.

In conclusion, social media has undeniably revolutionized the way we perceive and shape visual identity. It has democratized design, provided a platform for experimentation, and influenced our perception of authenticity. Whether you are an individual looking to establish your personal brand or a business aiming to create a recognizable image, harnessing the power of social media in shaping your visual identity is essential in today's digital landscape.

Predictions and Forecasts for Visual Identity in the Digital Age

As we enter the digital age, the power of creating a recognizable image has never been more important. In a world saturated with information, businesses and individuals need to stand out and make a lasting impression. In this subchapter, we will explore some predictions and forecasts for visual identity in the digital age, highlighting the significance of a recognizable image.

First and foremost, we can expect visual identity to play a crucial role in brand building. With the rise of social media and online platforms, companies will need to invest in creating a strong visual identity that resonates with their target audience. As technology continues to evolve, businesses will need to adapt their visual strategies to stay relevant and capture the attention of their customers.

One prediction is that personal branding will become even more important in the coming years. With the increasing popularity of influencers and content creators, individuals will need to establish a recognizable visual identity to stand out in a crowded digital landscape. Whether it's through a unique logo, consistent color scheme, or distinctive typography, individuals will have to strategically craft their visual identity to build a strong personal brand.

Another forecast is the integration of augmented reality (AR) and virtual reality (VR) into visual identity. As these technologies become more accessible, businesses will have the opportunity to create immersive brand experiences that go beyond traditional visual elements. Imagine being able to try on clothes virtually or see how furniture looks in your home before making a purchase. Visual identity will play a vital role in creating memorable and engaging experiences for customers.

Additionally, with the rise of artificial intelligence (AI), we can expect visual identity to become more personalized and adaptive. AI algorithms will analyze user preferences and behavior to deliver customized visual experiences. This means that businesses will need to constantly update and refine their visual identity to meet the ever-changing demands of their audience.

In conclusion, the digital age presents both challenges and opportunities for visual identity. As technology continues to advance, businesses and individuals must recognize the power of creating a recognizable image. By investing in a strong visual identity, companies can build brand loyalty, while individuals can establish a strong personal brand. Furthermore, the integration of AR, VR, and AI will push the boundaries of visual identity, allowing for more immersive and personalized experiences. As we move forward, it is essential for everyone to embrace the importance of visual identity in the digital age.

Chapter 10: Conclusion: Embracing Your Unique Visual Identity

Emphasizing the Value of Authenticity

In today's fast-paced and highly competitive world, creating a recognizable image is more crucial than ever. Whether you are an individual, a small business owner, or a large corporation, your visual identity plays a significant role in attracting and retaining customers. However, amidst the noise and clutter of the digital age, it's easy to fall into the trap of overediting and presenting a version of yourself or your brand that is not authentic. This is where emphasizing the value of authenticity becomes essential.

Authenticity is the key to establishing a genuine connection with your audience. It allows people to relate to you on a deeper level and builds trust, loyalty, and credibility. When your visual identity accurately reflects your values, personality, and purpose, it becomes a powerful tool that sets you apart from the competition.

In the age of filters and photo manipulation, it can be tempting to create a polished and picture-perfect image. However, authenticity lies in embracing imperfections and showing the real you. Your audience wants to see the genuine person behind the brand, flaws and all. By staying true to yourself and your values, you attract like-minded individuals who appreciate and resonate with your unique qualities.

One way to emphasize authenticity is by sharing your story. Every person and brand has a story to tell, and it is through storytelling that you can convey the essence of who you are and what you stand for.

Don't be afraid to reveal the challenges you've faced, the lessons you've learned, and the values that drive you. By doing so, you connect on a human level and create a sense of relatability that is invaluable in building lasting relationships.

Another aspect of authenticity is consistency. Your visual identity should be consistent across all platforms and communication channels. This ensures that people can recognize and remember you easily, reinforcing your brand image. Consistency also includes being transparent and honest in your interactions. Avoid misleading your audience with false claims or exaggerated promises. Instead, be genuine and deliver on your commitments, thereby building a strong foundation of trust.

Remember, the power of creating a recognizable image lies in its authenticity. Emphasizing this value not only sets you apart from the competition but also allows you to connect with your audience on a deeper level. So, embrace your uniqueness, share your story, and be consistent in your visual identity. By doing so, you will unleash the power of authenticity and create a lasting impression that resonates with everyone.

Taking Action to Unleash Your Visual Identity

In today's fast-paced world, establishing a strong visual identity has become more important than ever. With the rise of social media and the constant bombardment of information, it is essential to have a recognizable image that sets you apart from the crowd. Whether you are an individual or a business, creating a powerful visual identity can significantly impact your success.

The power of creating a recognizable image cannot be overstated. It is the first step towards building a strong brand and establishing your presence in the market. A visually appealing and consistent image helps you stand out, creates a sense of trust, and makes it easier for people to identify and remember you.

So, how can you take action to unleash your visual identity and harness its power? Here are some key steps to get you started:

1. Define Your Brand: Before you can create a visual identity, you need to understand your brand. What do you stand for? What values and qualities do you want to convey? Take the time to define your brand's personality and core message. This will guide your visual choices and ensure consistency across all platforms.

2. Design a Memorable Logo: Your logo is the cornerstone of your visual identity. It should be unique, memorable, and reflective of your brand. Consider hiring a professional designer to create a logo that captures the essence of your business or personal brand.

3. Choose Your Colors and Typography: Colors and typography play a crucial role in creating a recognizable image. Research color

psychology and choose a color palette that aligns with your brand's values and evokes the desired emotions. Similarly, select typography that complements your logo and enhances your message.

4. Consistency is Key: Once you have defined your brand and designed your visual elements, it is essential to maintain consistency across all platforms. Use your logo, colors, and typography consistently in your website, social media profiles, marketing materials, and any other touchpoints with your audience. This consistency will reinforce your brand image and make it easily recognizable.

5. Engage with Your Audience: Finally, actively engage with your audience to reinforce your visual identity. Share visually appealing content that reflects your brand's values and resonates with your target audience. Use your visual identity to tell a story and build a connection with your followers.

Remember, creating a recognizable visual identity is an ongoing process. Continuously evaluate and refine your brand image to ensure it remains relevant and impactful. By taking action and unleashing your visual identity, you will harness the power of a recognizable image and set yourself apart in today's competitive landscape.

Final Thoughts and Encouragement for Continued Growth

Congratulations! You have taken the first step towards harnessing the power of a recognizable image. Throughout this book, we have explored the importance of creating a visual identity that speaks to your audience and helps you stand out in a crowded marketplace. As we conclude this journey, let us reflect on the key takeaways and provide you with some encouragement for your continued growth.

The power of creating a recognizable image cannot be underestimated. In a world where attention spans are decreasing, it has become crucial to grab people's attention quickly and leave a lasting impression. Your visual identity serves as a powerful tool in achieving this goal. It allows you to communicate your brand's essence, values, and unique offerings in an instant.

Remember that your brand is more than just a logo or a color scheme; it encompasses your entire visual identity. From your website design to your packaging, every aspect should be cohesive and aligned with your brand's message. Consistency is key in establishing recognition and building trust with your audience. So, take the time to review your current visual elements and ensure they are consistently applied across all platforms.

Embrace the power of storytelling through visuals. Humans are wired to connect with stories, and visuals are a powerful medium to convey them. Use your visual identity to tell the story of your brand, its journey, and the people behind it. By doing so, you create an emotional connection with your audience, fostering loyalty and long-term relationships.

As you continue on your journey to unleash your visual identity, remember that growth is a continual process. Stay curious and open to new ideas and trends in the ever-evolving world of design and branding. Seek feedback from your audience and adapt accordingly. Experiment with different visual elements to see what resonates with your target market.

Finally, do not be afraid to take risks and be bold in your visual choices. The most memorable brands are often those that dare to be different. Embrace your uniqueness and let it shine through your visual identity. Have confidence in the power of your brand and its ability to make a lasting impact.

In conclusion, creating a recognizable image is a powerful tool in today's fast-paced world. Armed with the knowledge and insights gained from this book, you are now equipped to unleash your visual identity and make a lasting impression on your audience. Embrace the journey of continued growth, and remember that your brand has the potential to leave a mark in the hearts and minds of people.